New Curriculum

Primary Science
Learn, practise and revise

Year 6

Alan Jarvis and
William Merrick

RISING ★ STARS

Rising Stars UK Ltd, part of Hodder Education, an Hachette UK Company
Carmelite House, 50 Victoria Embankment, London, EC4Y 0DZ

www.risingstars-uk.com

Published 2013
Reprinted 2014, 2015 (twice)

Authors: Alan Jarvis and William Merrick

Science consultant: Shân Oswald, Improve Education

Text design: Green Desert Ltd

Cover design: West 8 Design

Illustrations: Oxford Designers and Illustrators; David Woodroffe

Publisher: Camilla Erskine

British Library Cataloguing in Publication Data.

A CIP record for this book is available from the British Library.

ISBN: 978-0-85769-685-4

Printed by Craft Print Pte Ltd, Singapore

Contents

How to use this book

How to get the best out of this book   4

Variation, adaptation and evolution

1   What are the five kingdoms?   6
2   What kinds of vertebrates are there?   8
3   How are plants adapted to where they live?   10
4   How are animals adapted to where they live?   12
5   Do plants and animals look like their parents?   14
6   How does variation help adaptation?   16
7   Which is best – four legs or two?   18
8   What does the fossil record tell us?   20
9   How do we know what lived long ago?   22
10   What is Darwin's theory of evolution?   24
11   How did Darwin make his discoveries?   26
12   How did our skeleton change as we evolved?   28

Blood circulation and staying healthy

13   What things are moved around inside your body?   30
14   What is your circulatory system for?   32
15   What does your heart do?   34
16   Who discovered blood circulation?   36
17   How are exercise and pulse rates linked?   38
18   How can we keep ourselves healthy?   40

Light

19   What is Newton's spectrum?   42
20   What do your eyes need to see things?   44
21   How does light travel?   46
22   How do light rays move?   48
23   What are reflections and shadows?   50
24   What can make white light change?   52

Electricity

25   What symbols are used in circuits?   54
26   Why do some circuits not work?   56
27   What happens when you change the components in a circuit?   58
28   What happens when cells change in a circuit?   60
29   What happens when you change the wires in a circuit?   62

Index   64

How to get the best out of this book

Each topic spreads across two pages and focuses on one major idea. Many of your lessons may be based on these topics. Each double page helps you to keep **On track** and **Aiming higher**.

Title and key ideas: tell you what you are aiming to learn. The second idea is always more difficult than the first.

Key information: sets out the key facts that you need to know and the ideas you need to understand fully.

Key questions: help you to learn more facts and understand the science in each topic. The investigations you do will give you the evidence you need to prove the scientific facts you've learnt.

Key words and their meanings: help build up your scientific vocabulary. Remember that some words mean one thing in everyday life and something more special in science.

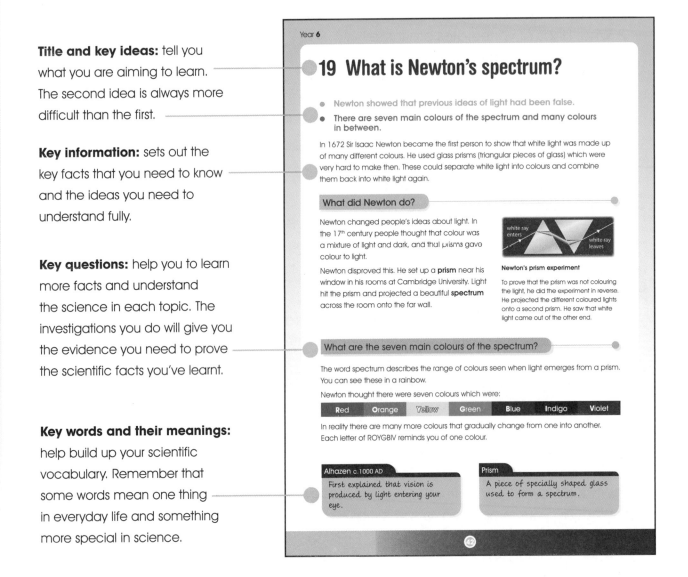

Year **6**

19 What is Newton's spectrum?

- Newton showed that previous ideas of light had been false.
- **There are seven main colours of the spectrum and many colours in between.**

In 1672 Sir Isaac Newton became the first person to show that white light was made up of many different colours. He used glass prisms (triangular pieces of glass) which were very hard to make then. These could separate white light into colours and combine them back into white light again.

What did Newton do?

Newton changed people's ideas about light. In the 17th century people thought that colour was a mixture of light and dark, and that prisms gave colour to light.

Newton disproved this. He set up a **prism** near his window in his rooms at Cambridge University. Light hit the prism and projected a beautiful **spectrum** across the room onto the far wall.

Newton's prism experiment

To prove that the prism was not colouring the light, he did the experiment in reverse. He projected the different coloured lights onto a second prism. He saw that white light came out of the other end.

What are the seven main colours of the spectrum?

The word spectrum describes the range of colours seen when light emerges from a prism. You can see these in a rainbow.

Newton thought there were seven colours which were:

| Red | Orange | Yellow | Green | Blue | Indigo | Violet |

In reality there are many more colours that gradually change from one into another. Each letter of ROYGBIV reminds you of one colour.

Alhazen c.1000 AD
First explained that vision is produced by light entering your eye.

Prism
A piece of specially shaped glass used to form a spectrum.

42

Follow these simple rules if you are using the book for revising.

1 Read each page carefully. Give yourself time to take in each idea.

2 Learn the key facts and ideas. Ask your teacher or mum, dad or the adult who looks after you if you need help.

3 Concentrate on the things you find more difficult.

4 Only work for about 20 minutes or so at a time. Take a break and then do more work.

The right-hand page has lots of fun questions for you to try. They help you to find how well you have understood what you have learned. There are questions on facts, ideas and scientific investigations. If you are stuck, the information on the left-hand page will help.

If you get most of the **On track** questions right then you are working at the expected level for the year. Well done – that's brilliant! If you get most of the **Aiming higher** questions right, you are working at the top of expectations for your year. You're doing really well!

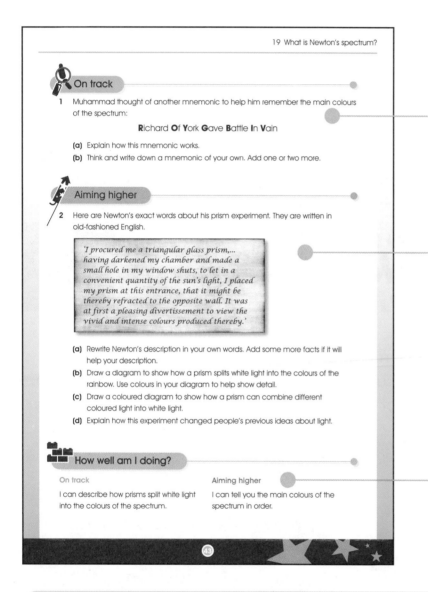

On track questions: come in different styles. Be sure to read each one carefully. Think about what the diagrams are telling you. Write your answers in your notebook.

Aiming higher questions: are more difficult. To answer them well, you have to know more facts or understand a harder idea. Write your answers in your notebook.

How well am I doing?: helps you to track progress. Keep a running record of how well you are doing so you keep on target.

Follow these simple rules if you want to know how well you are doing.

1 Work through the questions.

2 Check your answers with your teacher or using the answer booklet in the middle of the book.

3 Keep a record of how well you do.

4 Write down anything you are finding difficult and work through the chapter again to see if you can find the answer. If you are still finding it hard, ask your teacher for help.

1 What are the five kingdoms?

- Living things can be divided into five groups called kingdoms.
- **Each of the five kingdoms can be divided into smaller groups.**

Scientists put living things into groups with other similar ones. This is called classifying them. There are millions of different living things, so to start with they are classified into five big groups called **kingdoms**. Then each of those groups can be split again into smaller groups.

What are the five kingdoms?

These are the five big groups that contain all living things. The **bacteria** and the **protists** are very tiny; they can only be seen with a microscope.

Bacteria
Some 'germs' make us ill, but bacteria can be 'good' too. It can turn milk into yoghurt.

Protists
They are very tiny. Many live in ponds, and others live inside other living things.

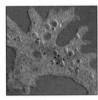

Fungi
Mushrooms and yeast have no leaves. They need food, e.g. dead wood and leaves, to survive.

Plants
Plants make their own food using sunlight energy. They cannot move on their own.

Animals
Creatures that can move on their own. They need to eat plants or other animals to survive.

Can the kingdoms be divided into smaller groups?

Vertebrates have backbones:

backbone

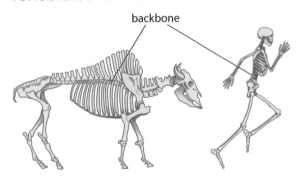

Invertebrates have no backbones at all:

A worm does not have a skeleton.

The snail has a shell on its back but no skeleton.

A crab's skeleton is on the outside. There are no bones inside!

Kingdom
One of the five main groups that animals can be put into.

Classify
To put plants and animals into groups with others that are similar to them.

On track

1 This key uses some facts about the five kingdoms.

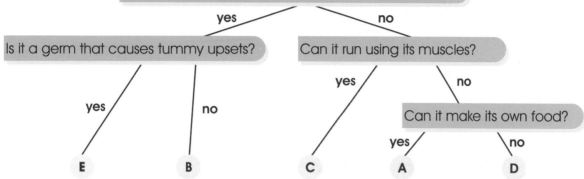

Is it so small it can only be seen with a microscope?

yes — no

Is it a germ that causes tummy upsets? Can it run using its muscles?

yes — no   yes — no

Can it make its own food?

yes — no

E   B   C   A   D

(a) Write the names of these five living things and mark each one with the letter (A–E) from above that belongs to it.

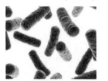  

E. coli:	amoeba:	fox:	mushroom:	buttercup:
a bacterium	a protist	an animal	a fungus	a plant

Aiming higher

2 On the previous page you can see pictures of two vertebrates, and three invertebrates. They have been put into a chart for you.

Vertebrates	Invertebrates
Cow	Worm
Human	Snail
	Crab

Draw out the table, and see how many extra animals you can put into the columns. Think about animals you know in your ordinary life – animals on the farm, in the zoo, in the park or in the garden.

How well am I doing?

On track

I can name the five main kingdoms of living things.

Aiming higher

I can explain the difference between vertebrates and invertebrates.

2 What kinds of vertebrates are there?

- The animals with backbones can be divided into five main groups.
- Each of those main groups can be divided into a number of smaller groups.

Fish and cats share a very important feature. They both have backbones, so they are both **vertebrates**. There are important differences as well, so we put them in different groups of vertebrates. There are five groups of vertebrates altogether.

What different kinds of animal have backbones?

Animals with **cold** blood. It is the same temperature inside their bodies as the world around them.	**Fish:**	• covered in scales • live in water all the time • lay eggs in the water.	
	Amphibians:	• smooth moist skin • live partly in water and partly on land • lay eggs in the water.	
	Reptiles:	• dry scaly skin • live on land but some can swim • hatch from eggs laid on land.	
Animals with **warm** blood. They always stay the same temperature inside.	**Birds:**	• have feathers • most can fly • hatch from eggs.	
	Mammals:	• have hair • babies grow inside the mother • mother makes milk to feed the babies.	

What are the three types of mammals?

Placental mammals

Babies grow inside the mother until they are strong enough to survive.

Marsupials

Babies are born when very tiny, and feed and grow inside the mother's pouch.

Monotremes

The duck-billed platypus from Australia lays eggs that hatch out later.

Feature

Something that can be used to identify a living thing and put it into a group.

Backbone

Also called the spine. The row of bones down the back that supports the animal.

On track

1   This key shows the differences between different animals with backbones.

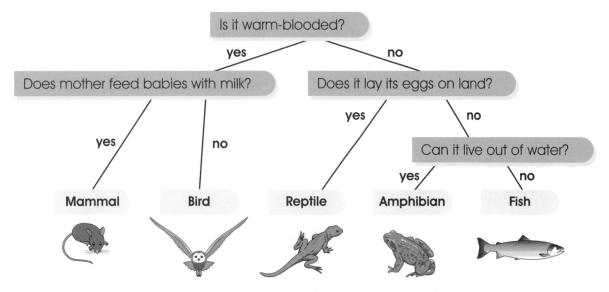

(a) Which type of animal is warm-blooded and feeds its babies with milk?

(b) What two kinds of animal in the key lay their eggs in water?

(c) Can an amphibian live out of the water?

Aiming higher

2   Sally was classifying these mammals. She decided they belonged to three different groups.

  Duck-billed platypus   Kangaroo    Mouse

(a) What features do they all have in common?

(b) The platypus is a **monotreme**. What is the main feature that puts it in that group?

(c) What other feature can you see that makes the platypus an unusual mammal?

(d) What feature could be used to separate the kangaroo (**a marsupial**) and the mouse (**a placental mammal**)?

How well am I doing?

On track

I can explain the difference between the five groups of animals with backbones.

Aiming higher

I can explain how the three groups of mammals are different.

3 How are plants adapted to where they live?

- Every different habitat has some difficulties that the plants need to deal with.

- **Plants all have special features that let them survive in their own habitat.**

There are many different kinds of place where plants can live. All of those different places to live are called **habitats**. Each habitat has its own set of plants which have special **adaptations** to living there.

What difficulties are there in different habitats?

The **desert** is very hot and there is hardly any water.

Plants need light to make food and to grow. A **forest** is dark under the trees so not much grows on the ground.

How are some plants adapted to difficult habitats?

- A **cactus** can store water in its thick stem.
- It has spines instead of leaves to prevent water escaping, and also to stop animals biting into it to steal water.

- In **spring** the leaves grow on the trees and make it shady in the forest.
- Bluebells grow right at the beginning of spring, before the leaves make it too dark.

Habitat

The place where an animal or plant lives, giving it food, water and shelter.

Adaptation

A special feature of an animal or plant that lets it live in a certain habitat.

On track

1   Some cows are grazing in Farmer Brown's meadow. They mainly eat grass. Mixed up with the grass are other tasty plants like clover and buttercups.

Here are some facts about the meadow habitat.

- There is lots of sunshine.
- The cows walk on the plants.
- There is lots of rain.
- The cows eat the grass, clover and buttercups.
- The cows use the field as a toilet.

Some of those facts are good for the plants, and some make it harder for them to live in the meadow. Sort them into two lists in this table.

Things that make it **easy** for plants to live in a meadow	Things that make it **hard** for plants to live in a meadow

Aiming higher

2   A plant that survives well in a meadow is the thistle. The cows eat the grass all around it, but they leave the thistle alone.

Young thistles look like this.

They grow up to this.

Name two adaptations the thistle has that let it live safely in a cow meadow.

How well am I doing?

On track

I can describe some things in a habitat that make it easy or hard for plants to survive.

Aiming higher

I can explain how plants are adapted to survive in their habitat.

4 How are animals adapted to where they live?

- Every different habitat has some difficulties that the animals need to deal with.

- Animals all have special features that let them survive in their own habitat.

Just like plants, animals have to struggle to survive in their own habitats. They all have special ways of doing that. Animals that are hunted by others can usually run fast, and may have patterns and colours that help them to hide from the hunters.

What different habitats are there?

The plains of Africa

The Arctic ice

Under the sea

A forest

How are animals adapted to their habitats?

A duck's body is just right to live in water. Its feathers are waterproof and its webbed feet help it to swim.

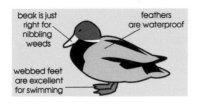

beak is just right for nibbling weeds

feathers are waterproof

webbed feet are excellent for swimming

The tiger is **camouflaged**. Its stripes help it to hide when it is hunting.

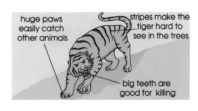

huge paws easily catch other animals

stripes make the tiger hard to see in the trees

big teeth are good for killing

Camouflage
Colours and patterns that help animals blend into their background.

Webs
The skin in between a duck's toes that helps it to push against the water.

On track

1   Here are four habitats:

| plains of Africa | Arctic ice | forest | Atlantic Ocean |

Copy this table. Use the pictures on the opposite page to describe the habitat. The first one is done for you.

Habitat	Main features
Plains of Africa	Hot and dry without much shelter Mostly grassland

Aiming higher

2   The polar bear is adapted to live in the cold Arctic lands around the North Pole.

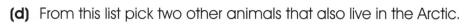

(a)   Why is it covered with thick fur?

(b)   Why do you think it is white in colour?

(c)   How do you think its very big paws help it to survive?

(d)   From this list pick two other animals that also live in the Arctic.

| seal | lion | kangaroo | reindeer |

How well am I doing?

On track

I can name at least four different habitats and say what they are like.

Aiming higher

I can explain how some animals are adapted to live in their environment.

5 Do plants and animals look like their parents?

- All plants and animals have babies the same kind as themselves.
- **Baby animals and new plants are sometimes slightly different from their parents.**

Dogs never have kittens, and cats don't have puppies. Babies are the same kind as the parents. It's the same with plants. Plant the seeds from a pea plant and you get more peas, not beans! But the kittens in a litter are not all exactly the same.

Do animals and plants look like their relatives?

This is just what we expect. The calf (baby) looks like her mum and dad.

When this pine sapling grows, it will look a lot like the full-grown ones behind.

Are babies exactly the same as their parents?

These kittens have the same parents. There are differences between them. They are **similar** but not the **same**.

It is true for plants, too. They are the same kind as their parents, but there can be differences in size, colour and shape.

Same

When two things are exactly the same you can't easily tell them apart. Identical twins look the same.

Similar

Two things that are similar are alike, but not exactly. Parents and their children look **similar** to each other.

On track

Peter and Susan have three children: Jim, Mary and John. Everybody can tell they are brothers and sisters. They are not **exactly** the same, though.

| Peter | Susan | Jim | Mary | John |

Look carefully at the pictures of the family. Each child got some features from their mum and some from their dad. They didn't all get the same ones.

1   Show which features came from each parent by copying the table below. The first line has been done for you.

(a)

	Jim	Mary	John
Hair colour	From dad	From dad	From mum
Hair (straight or curly)			
Eye colour			
Freckles			

(b) Which feature has Peter given to all three children?

(c) Which feature has Susan given to all three children?

(d) Are any of the children exactly the same as their parents?

Aiming higher

2   The brother and sister are similar but not the same.

    (a) Write down two things that tell you they are related – ways they look alike.

    (b) Write down two ways you can tell them apart – ways they look different.

How well am I doing?

On track

I can describe ways that animals and plants are similar to their parents, and to their brothers and sisters.

Aiming higher

I can describe the ways that animals and plants may be different from their parents.

6 How does variation help adaptation?

- The children in a family look similar but they are not exactly the same.

- **Small differences could make a big difference to survival.**

Sally and Jane are sisters. They look like each other, but not exactly. Sally has her mum's brown hair, but Jane is blond like her dad. Sally likes sport and can run faster than Jane.

Why are brothers and sisters different?

Babies might **inherit** a different mixture of features from their two parents. Cat parents always have cat babies, but they might be different in small ways.

With a ginger father and a black and white mother, a litter of kittens will contain both types.

We all inherit our looks from our parents, but there is **variation** in what we inherit.

The adaption process

Small inherited differences could help some animals and plants to survive better than others. The differences might make them better **adapted.**

Having big flat feet is an **adaptation** to walking in the desert. A camel's feet stop it sinking into the soft sand.

A camel born with slightly bigger feet might find it easier to survive than the others. It will be better **adapted** than the others.

The yellow colour and the pattern attract the bee to the flower. It is an **adaptation** to insect pollination.

Flowers that are brighter and with a stronger pattern will attract more bees.

If the camels with the biggest feet are always the ones to survive, in the end they will all have big feet. And all the flowers will be brightly coloured and patterned. Both species will have changed to become better adapted.

Variation	Adaptations
The slight differences between different creatures of the same type.	Features inherited from our parents that help us survive.

On track

1   Ms Rankin showed Panther class how to measure round their heads.

They counted how many children had each measurement.

They put their results in a table.

Distance round head (circumference)	Numbers of children
52 cm	1
53 cm	7
54 cm	10
55 cm	6
56 cm	2

(a) What was the smallest head size?

(b) How many children had the largest head size?

(c) What was the most common head size?

(d) Make a bar chart to show the results.

Aiming higher

2   Mammoths were very much like elephants, but they lived in cold and snowy places. They died out about 10,000 years ago.

Modern elephants now live in hotter places like India and Africa.

A modern Indian elephant   A woolly mammoth

(a) What adaptation helped mammoths to survive in cold places?

(b) An animal's behaviour can be adapted as well as its body. What is the elephant in the picture doing that helps it stay cool in a hot climate?

(c) Other animals that live in cold climates often have small noses and ears. How do you think that might help them to survive?

(d) Now you have answered part c), look again at the pictures of the elephant and the mammoth. Can you now explain why the mammoth has small ears and the elephant has big ones?

How well am I doing?

On track

I can describe the variation between members of the same species.

Aiming higher

I can explain how variation helps plants and animals become adapted.

7 Which is best – four legs or two?

- Most mammals walk on four legs, but humans walk on only two.
- **There must be some reasons why people walk on only two legs.**

Have you ever wondered why human beings only walk on two legs? Most of the other mammals use all four legs all of the time. Walking on two legs and having our arms free must help us in some way. It must be an **adaptation** to help us survive.

What makes four legs good?

There are some jobs that four-legged animals (**quadrupeds**) are well **adapted** to do. They are very good at some things – much better than humans sometimes.

Four-legged animals are safer from falling over.

Having four legs helps horses run very fast.

Predators use four legs with claws to catch their prey.

Are there special reasons for going on two legs?

Some mammals that normally use four legs can stand on their back legs for a little while, just to do special things. Human beings are good at those things too.

Meerkats stand up so they can see what is coming.

Squirrels can balance on two legs to hold nuts.

Chimpanzees use their arms and hands to care for their babies.

We have good brains to invent useful things, but we need hands to be able to make and use these things.

Bipedal

Walking on **two** legs. "Bi" means "two" and "ped" means "feet".

Quadripedal

Walking on **four** legs. "Quad" means "four".

On track

1   Most mammals walk on four legs.

(a) What advantages do animals that walk on four legs have compared to human beings with only two?

(b) Why is it safer for a human baby to use four legs to start with?

Aiming higher

2   Human beings walk on two legs all the time. Some mammals do the same thing, just at special times. Standing up on two legs is an **adaptation** to help us in many ways. Here are some of the advantages (helpful things).

It lets us hold our babies to look after them.	We can use weapons like bows and arrows for hunting.
It lets us use our hands to use tools to make things and grow food.	It helps us see further to spot danger coming.
We can pick up food to eat it with our hands.	We can carry things we have made with us.

(a) Copy out this table and use it to sort the advantages into two lists: one list of things that just help humans, and one list of things that help a few other mammals as well. The first one has been done for you.

Things that help people and a few other mammals	Things that just help people
It lets us hold our babies to look after them.	

(b) Are there any things people are worse at because we walk on two legs?

How well am I doing?

On track

I know that most mammals walk on four legs.

Aiming higher

I can explain that walking on two legs is an **adaptation** for some special things humans can do.

8 What does the fossil record tell us?

- Fossils in rocks show us what plants and animals were like in the past.
- **The fossils in the older rocks are different from modern animals and plants.**

The remains of plants and animals buried under layers of rock show what used to live on the Earth. The deeper they are buried, the older they are. Looking back in time, we see we see very different animals and plants.

Where are the oldest fossils?

Newer fossils

Older fossils

- This area was under water for millions of years. Mud, sand and other sorts of sediment settled on the bed and built up the rock layers.
- Animals and plants were trapped in those layers and became fossils.
- The **newest** fossils are on top, **near the surface**. The **oldest** fossils are **the deepest**.

How do older fossils differ from modern plants and animals?

5,000 years ago

Near the surface we find the remains of plants and animals not very different from the ones alive today.	People who looked a lot like us hunted mammoths. The plants were more or less the same as the ones we have now.

66 million years ago

In deeper rocks we see that things were very different. Dinosaurs ruled the Earth – but were just about to die out.	There were some small mammals but no humans yet. Mosses, ferns and conifers were found. Flowering plants began to appear.

530 million years ago

Most life was found in the sea. On land the first few animals were a little like centipedes.	The sea contained worms and jellyfish. No fish yet. On land the plants were like mosses.

Dinosaur

Reptiles that died out millions of years ago. The word means "Terrible Lizard".

Extinct

Animals and plants that have all died out are extinct.

You can use this chart to answer all of the questions on this page.

Millions of years ago	Fish	Amphibians	Reptiles	Birds	Mammals
1					humans
10				modern birds	horses, dogs, primates
100			crocodiles dinosaurs end		pigs, deer, cats, rodents
150				first birds	
200		early frogs	dinosaurs turtles	×	small mammals
250				×	×
300			small reptiles	×	×
350			×	×	×
400	sharks and bony fish	first amphibians	×	×	×
450		×	×	×	×
500	early fish	×	×	×	×

On track

1 These questions are about hunting for fossils in layers of rock.

(a) What fossils would you find in the deepest layers of rock?

(b) Which layers would you look in for the fossils of human beings?

Aiming higher

2 (a) What sorts of vertebrates were alive 400 million years ago?

(b) We often see a cartoon of a caveman with a dinosaur.
Explain why this could never really have happened.

(c) Put these types of animals in order starting with the first ones to appear:

mammals   fish   birds   reptiles   amphibians

How well am I doing?

On track

I know the deepest fossils are the oldest.

Aiming higher

I know that different animals and plants appeared at different times.

9 How do we know what lived long ago?

- We know what lived millions of years ago from digging up fossils.
- **We work out what the animals looked like from their bones and shells.**

Who was a famous fossil hunter?

Mary Anning was a famous British fossil hunter. She lived in Lyme Regis in Dorset about 200 years ago.

The cliffs near there are from the **Jurassic** period, and they contain dinosaur skeletons. Mary earned a living by finding the skeletons, digging them up and selling them. Famous scientists visited her to buy fossils.

In those days women could not study at college or get jobs as scientists, so Mary had to teach herself about fossils.

How do the bones show us the shape of the animals?

Fossils are usually just bones, or rocks in the shape of the bones that were once there. Usually there is nothing left of the muscles or skin, so scientists have to try to work out what the living animal might have looked like.

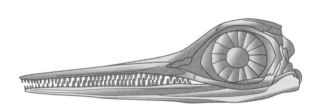

Mary's brother Joseph found this ichthyosaur skull, and Mary found the rest of the body. It was the first one ever found.

This is what we think ichthyosaurs were like. They look like dolphins, but dolphins are mammals. Ichthyosaurs were reptiles.

Fossils

Traces of animals and plants that have been dug up. We may find bones or shells, or just the prints of them in the rock.

Jurassic

A time from 213 million years ago to 144 million years ago. Some famous Jurassic creatures were **stegosaurs** on land and **ichthyosaurs** in the sea.

On track

1   Mary Anning's discoveries were very important because they came at a time when scientists were finding out about the age of the Earth and what lived on it long ago.

Here are some facts about the events of Mary's life. They are not in order.

> **1811** Mary (aged 12) finds first *Ichthyosaur* in Britain.
>
> **1828** Mary finds a flying reptile *Pterosaurus.*
>
> **1833** Mary nearly killed by a rock fall while digging.
>
> **1800** Baby Mary survives being struck by lightning!
>
> **1823** Mary finds first *Plesiosaurus* (a sea dinosaur).

Draw out the timeline shown on the right and put these events on to it.

1850	
1845	Mary died 1847
1840	
1835	
1830	
1825	
1820	
1815	
1810	
1805	
1800	
1795	Mary born 1795

Aiming higher

2   Mary Anning's life was also important because it showed that women could be good at science, and many other things as well. Now there are many women scientists, but Mary was one of the first.

Here are some more recent facts about the history of women. They are not in order.

1903 Marie Curie wins Nobel Prize for Physics.

1991 Helen Sharman becomes the first British female astronaut.

1918 Women over 30 first allowed to vote.

1979 Margaret Thatcher becomes first female British prime minister. She had a science degree.

1953 Rosalind Franklin helps discover shape of DNA.

2000	
1975	
1950	
1925	
1900	

Draw out the timeline shown on the right and use it to put these events in the right order.

How well am I doing?

On track

I can describe some ancient creatures and their fossils.

Aiming higher

I can explain how we work out what ancient animals looked like by studying their skeletons.

10 What is Darwin's theory of evolution?

- Farmers have bred better types of animal and plant for their farms.
- Darwin thought that nature could also slowly change plants and animals.

Darwin said that older types of plant and animal found in **fossils** had **gradually changed** into the modern ones, little bit at a time. That slow change is called **evolution**. He thought it worked by a process called **natural selection**.

How do farmers change animals and plants?

Farm animals and plants have been changed by farmers. Cows give more milk than they used to. Farm potatoes are much bigger than wild ones.

Variation gives farmers different types to pick from. They **select** the ones they like best to be parents of the next generation, and slowly the species changes. This is called **artificial selection**.

All the tame dogs we know today have been bred from wolves. To get smaller dogs people kept on choosing the smaller puppies to be the next parents.

How does it work in nature?

Darwin said that **nature** selected animals and plants to breed from.

- In nature there is a **struggle for survival**. Many die when young.
- Only animals or plants with the best adaptations will survive. This is the **survival of the fittest**.
- The survivors become the parents of the next generation, and their babies **inherit** the useful adaptation.
- The species has begun to change. This is called **evolution** by **natural selection**.

Longer-necked giraffes survived to have babies because they could get more food. Soon all the giraffes inherited long necks.

Survival of the fittest

The way that the best adapted animals and plants live to breed.

Evolution

The slow and gradual change of one form of life to another.

On track

1   Read these facts about some types of dog, which were all bred from wolves in the first place.

Greyhounds have got long legs, can breathe very well and run fast.

Labradors have a very good sense of smell.

King Charles Spaniels are small and friendly and they don't bite.

(a) Which type of dog would make the best pet for a child to keep at home?

(b) Which type would be the best to help firemen find people trapped in a building that has fallen down in an earthquake?

(c) Which would be the best dog to race against other dogs?

(d) People bred husky dogs to pull their sledges in the snowy and cold lands in the North.

  • What would they have been looking for when deciding which puppies be the parents of the next generation?

Aiming higher

2   Look at the picture. The zebra is in danger, but so is the lion! The zebra's very hard kick can break a lion's jaw. Also, if the zebras are too quick and get away the lion will starve.

(a) What adaptations has the lion got that help it survive?

(b) What slight differences might there be between two lions that might help one survive better than the other?

(c) Explain how lions might have all come to be the same sandy yellow colour.

How well am I doing?

On track

I can describe how people can breed new types of animals and plants.

Aiming higher

I can explain how new types are produced in nature.

11 How did Darwin make his discoveries?

- Some people already realised that the world was very old, and that plants and animals were different long ago to the ones we have now.

- Darwin produced a clear explanation of evolution, with plenty of evidence.

Charles Darwin puzzled over two really big questions:

- Where did all the different living things on the planet come from?
- How did they come to be adapted to survive?

What did he know to start him off?

- Charles knew the work of scientists such as Mary Anning, so he knew that fossils showed us that animals and plants were different long ago.
- He knew that people had bred better farm animals and food crops. Selecting which ones to breed from could slowly change a species.
- His own grandfather, **Erasmus Darwin**, had a similar idea about evolution years earlier, but didn't have any evidence to prove it.

How did he collect his evidence?

Charles was a scientist on board a Royal Navy ship. It was on a voyage to explore the coast of South America and make maps for the Navy.

His ship the *HMS Beagle* sailed to the remote **Galapagos Islands** in 1831.

There are many types of finches found only on those islands. They are **adapted** for different ways of life.

- Number 1 cracks seeds with its big strong beak.
- Number 4 spears insects with its sharp pointed one.

Charles thought that just one type had arrived on the island long ago, which had then **evolved** into the many new types. This was a sign that evolution had happened in nature.

Galapagos Islands
A group of islands off the West coast of South America.

Remote
A long way away from other places.

On track

1   Read this passage about the discovery of evolution, and then set out the information on a timeline.

You will need a timeline that starts in 1800 and runs up to 1860.

Darwin was not the first scientist to think about evolution. Darwin's famous book, the Origin of Species, was published in 1859. A lot had happened before that. In 1858 Alfred Wallace published the idea in partnership with Darwin. Erasmus Darwin explained some early thoughts about it in 1803 in a poem. A Frenchman called Lamarck gave a lecture in favour of it 1800. In 1811 Mary and her brother Joseph discovered the skeleton of a dinosaur called Ichthyosaurus.

Aiming higher

Since Darwin's time many fossils have been found which show how different animals have evolved. Fossil horse bones give us evidence for evolution.

2   Fossils of horses like the ones we have today are found in fairly new rocks from about 1 million years ago.
In rocks 5 million years old there are no horse bones. We find some smaller animals that would have looked quite like horses.
50 million years ago there was nothing very much like a horse, but some dog-sized animals had interesting middle toes!

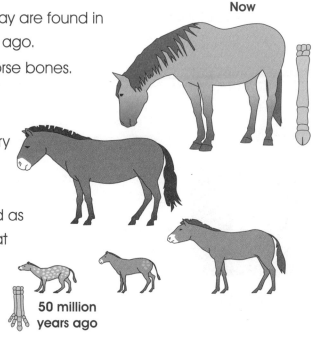

Now

50 million years ago

(a) Describe the changes that happened as the horse slowly took shape during that 50 million years. Think about the size and shape of the whole animal.

(b) How do you think those changes to the horses' legs might have helped them to survive better?

How well am I doing?

On track

I know that fossils show us that plants and animals living long ago were different to today.

Aiming higher

I can explain how evolution is caused by natural selection.

12 How did our skeleton change as we evolved?

- Human beings evolved from ancient primates over millions of years.
- The human skeleton has **adaptations to help us survive.**

'Cave people' who looked a lot like us and made stone tools were quite recent. They were painting in caves about 20,000 years ago. Before them comes a long story of gradual change.

Where and when did humans first appear?

The earliest human fossils are found in Africa. We began to expand out of Africa and settle in the rest of the world only about 60,000 years ago.

The journey from ape to human took 25 million years!

- The earliest fossils of humans with skeletons **exactly** like ours are found from about 200,000 years ago.

- Upright types that were similar but less tall and with smaller brains are found between 1 and 3 million years ago.

What is our skeleton adapted for?

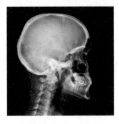 We are **intelligent**, so we need a large skull for our brains.

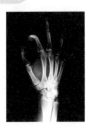 Our hands are important too, as they let us make and use **tools**. We can make better use of our big brains because of our gripping hands.

We are **bipedal**. We walk upright on two legs. This sets our hands free to use tools, and also lets us see further.

- Our legs bones are **long** to walk faster and see further.
- Our hips and knees are **strong** to take our whole weight.
- Our hips are **wide** to fix the walking muscles to.
- Our spine is more **curved** to act as a shock absorber.

Homo sapiens	Bipedal
The human species. "Homo" = "mankind" and "sapiens = "wise".	Able to walk on two legs.

On track

1   This is a modern chimpanzee. It is **not** our ancestor, but it has a skeleton similar to ours which has not been adapted to walk upright on two legs.

(a)   Make a list of differences you can see between the chimpanzee skeleton and ours.

(b)   Go on to the Internet or look in school library books to find out more about some of our early ancestors. What names have we given them? Where and when did they live? What did they look like? What fossils have been found?

Aiming higher

2   Sort these adaptations of humans skeletons into the two groups set out below:

The skull has a large brain case.	Arms and hands are not needed to walk with.
Hands have thumbs that can grip.	Strong hip and knee bones
Wide hips to attach leg muscles to.	A curved spine with some spring in it

(a)   Group 1: Adaptations to walking upright

(b)   Group 2: Adaptations to greater intelligence and using tools

How well am I doing?

On track

I can describe how the human skeleton changed as we evolved.

Aiming higher

I can explain how those changes allowed us to become more intelligent and use tools.

13 What things are moved around inside your body?

● Dissolved food and water is moved from the intestines to all parts of the body.

● **The blood carries those and other things from place to place inside the body**

Have you ever wondered what your blood is actually for? An adult has about 4 litres of it, and if you lose too much in an accident you could even die!

What has to be moved around the body?

This picture shows the stomach and intestines. That is where the food goes when you eat it. The stomach and intestines dissolve the food you have eaten.

The muscles, and all the rest of the body too, need that food and water to stay alive. The food gives the muscles the **energy** they need to move. They need a constant supply of food and water.

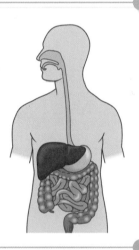

What does the blood do?

● **It carries the food and water.**

There is blood in every part of your body. Wherever you cut yourself, some blood will come out.

Blood can pick up the food and water from your intestine and take it to the rest of your body.

● **It helps to keep you warm.**

Blood carries heat from warm parts, like muscles, to cold parts, like fingers and toes and nose. The red cheeks and nose are caused by extra blood keeping them warm!

Intestines
The long tube inside your body that digests your food.

Blood
The red liquid that carries dissolved food and water around your body.

On track

1   This picture shows the insides of a human being.

   (a) What are the names of the parts A, B and C?

   You can pick from *stomach*, *muscles* and *intestine*.

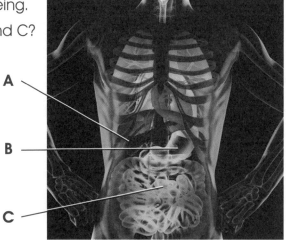

   (b) Which of those three parts do these jobs?
   - Dissolve the food
   - Hold the food when it is first swallowed
   - Move the body

Aiming higher

2   These words are all to do with the jobs your blood does for you.

| blood clot | intestines | fingers | muscles |

Copy and complete this table using the words above.

This seals up a cut to keep germs out.	
A part of your body that makes heat when you run.	
Where food and water enters the blood.	
A part of your body that gets very cold in winter.	

How well am I doing?

On track

I can describe how the circulatory system carries blood to connect all parts of the body.

Aiming higher

I can describe some of the jobs that the circulatory system does.

14 What is your circulatory system for?

- All parts of the body are connected by tubes called blood vessels.
- **The circulatory system carries blood to all parts of the body.**

The blood in your body runs around in tubes called blood vessels. All of the blood vessels are connected, and the blood just keeps travelling round and round your body inside them. Every part of your body gets a visit as it runs round, so that is why the blood can deliver things from one part to another.

What are blood vessels?

The tubes of the **circulatory system** connect every part of the body. Blood moves round it all the time.

In some places the tubes are just under the skin and you can see them quite easily.

The tubes are called **blood vessels**. Inside them are **red blood cells**, which give blood its red colour.

The cells are floating in a liquid called **plasma**. Plasma carries the water and dissolved food along.

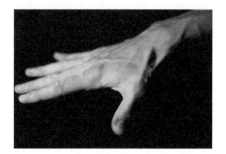

What is blood circulation?

All of the blood vessels are connected in a loop that runs all around the body.

It takes your blood round and round, so it visits every part of you over and over again. It never stops running for your whole life!

When the blood visits the intestines it can pick up the water and dissolved food. It then moves on round the circulatory system, carrying them along in the blood.

As it runs through the muscles it can deliver some food and water to them.

Then it returns to the intestines to collect some more.

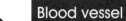

Circulation

This is related to the word "circle". It describes the way blood goes round and round the body.

Blood vessel

These are the tubes that carry your blood. They all join up into one big loop.

RISING STARS

Science Study Guide: Year 6

Answer Booklet

Unit		On track		Aiming higher
1 What are the five kingdoms?	1	A – buttercup B – amoeba C – fox D – mushroom E – E. coli	2	*Own answers*
2 What kind of vertebrates are there?	1(a) (b) (c)	A mouse Amphibian and fish Yes	2(a) (b) (c) (d)	Features in common: hair, warm blood, mothers make milk The platypus lays eggs that hatch out later. The platypus has a bill like a duck. Placental mammals have a pouch.
3 How are plants adapted to where they live?	1	Things that make it easy for plants to live in a meadow: There is lots of sunshine; There is lots of rain; The cows use the field as a toilet. Things that make it hard for plants to live in a meadow: The cows walk on the plants; The cows eat the grass, clover and buttercups.	2	The thistle grows very flat on the ground when young and when it grows taller it is covered in prickly leaves.
4 How are animals adapted to where they live?	1	Arctic ice: Cold and covered in snow and ice. No vegetation. Forest: Covered in large trees with some clearings. Atlantic Ocean: Deep salt water.	2(a) (b) (c) (d)	Thick fur to help keep it warm. To help blend into its surroundings (camouflage). To provide grip/to help kill seals/to swim better/to avoid sinking into the snow. Seal and reindeer
5 Do plants and animals look like their parents?	1(a)		2(a) (b)	Suitable answers include: hair colour/eye colour/face shape. The boy is larger and has shorter hair.

Table for question 5 1(a):

	Jim	Mary	John
Hair colour	dad	dad	mum
Straight or curly	dad	dad	dad
Eye colour	dad	dad	mum
Freckles	mum	mum	mum

Unit		On track		Aiming higher
	(b) (c) (d)	Peter has given straight hair to all the children. Susan gas given freckles to all of the children. No		
6 How does variation help adaptation?	1(a) (b) (c) (d)	52cm 2 54cm A suitable chart	2(a) (b) (c) (d)	Mammoths had long woolly coats. It is squirting water over its back. They don't lose very much heat through their nose and ears. The mammoth has small ears to reduce heat loss.

Unit		On track		Aiming higher	
7 Which is better – four legs or two?	1(a) (b)	Having four legs allows greater stability and speed. To reduce the chance of falling over.	2(a)	**Things that help people and a few other mammals**	**Things that just help people**
				It lets us hold our babies to look after them.	It lets us use our hands to use tools to make things and grow food.
				It helps us see further to spot danger coming.	We can use weapons like bows and arrows for hunting.
				We can pick up food to eat it with our hands.	We can carry things we have made with us.
			(b)	Running and balancing.	
8 What does the fossil record tell us?	1(a) (b)	Early fish Rocks nearest the surface/most recent rocks.	2(a) (b) (c)	Sharks and bony fish, first amphibians. Dinosaurs died out before the first humans appeared. Fish → amphibians → reptiles → mammals → birds	
9 How do we know what lived long ago?	1(a)	A suitable timeline	2(a)	A suitable timeline	
10 What is Darwin's theory of evolution?	1(a) (b) (c) (d)	King Charles Spaniel Labrador Greyhound Strong and fast with thick fur	2(a) (b) (c)	Adaptations: camouflage colours, strength, teeth, claws Suitable answers include hunting adaptations. Lions born a different colour would not blend into their surroundings so prey would see them coming and they wouldn't catch any food.	
11 How did Darwin make his discoveries?	1	A suitable timeline	2(a) (b)	A suitable description explaining how the horse grew larger, the legs lengthened, the foot changed and the hoof is modified into a single toenail. These are adaptations to running on grassy surfaces.	
12 How did our skeleton change as we evolved?	1(a) (b)	Suitable answers include: The chimp is less adapted to walk upright – stooping posture. Long front legs can act as walking legs. The skull of chimp is heavier, with bigger jaws and teeth *Own answers*	2(a) (b)	**Group 1**	**Group 2**
				Wide hips to attach leg muscles to.	The skull has a large brain case.
				Strong hip and knee bones.	Hands have thumbs that can grip.
				A curved spine with some spring in it.	Arms and hands are not needed to walk with.
13 What things are moved around inside your body?	1(a) (b)	A – muscle B – stomach C – intestine Dissolve the food – C Hold the food when it is first swallowed – B Move the body – A	2(a)	This seals up a cut to keep germs out.	blood clot
				A part of your body that makes heat when you run.	muscles
				Where food can water enters the blood.	intestines
				A part of your body that gets very cold in winter.	fingers

Unit		On track		Aiming higher
14 What is your circulatory system for?	**1(a)**	The blood had run downwards away from the 'up' hand and into the 'down' hand.	**2(a)**	We eat some food → Our intestines dissolve the food → Blood collects dissolved food from the intestines → Blood carries dissolved food to the muscles → The muscles use the dissolved food to work → We can move around → Blood returns to intestines.
15 What does your heart do?	**1(a)** **(b)** **(c)** **(d)**	Muscle Pumps blood around the body Circulates Exercise/eat a healthy diet/do not smoke.	**2(a)** **(b)** **(c)** **(d)** **(e)** **(f)**	2 minutes 8 minutes Will Jamal Will Will
16 Who discovered blood circulation?	**1(a)**	A suitable timeline	**2(a)** **(b)**	A suitable timeline Harry did an experiment that showed blood always flowed in the same direction. Galen did not know blood circulated.
17 How are exercise and pulse rates linked?	**1**	<table><tr><th>Question</th><th>Answer</th></tr><tr><td>What pushes blood through your blood vessels?</td><td>The heart</td></tr><tr><td>Where can you feel your pulse?</td><td>In your wrist</td></tr><tr><td>What is a normal pulse rate for somebody sitting quietly?</td><td>100</td></tr><tr><td>What is the blood taking to your muscles?</td><td>Dissolved food</td></tr></table>	**2(a)** **(b)**	Lying down resting for ten minutes – Dylan Sitting in a chair doing some writing – Sally Walking slowly – Mina Running really fast – Felix Using the same person each time makes sure differences are due to different levels of activity rather than individual fitness.
18 How can we keep ourselves healthy?	**1(a)** **(b)** **(c)**	Healthy weight Overweight Suitable answers include: eat less/ eat healthily/exercise	**2(a)** **(b)**	Suitable answers include: It damages the heart and lungs/ can cause illness/makes you unfit/ expensive Smoking is addictive
19 What is Newton's spectrum?	**1(a)** **(b)**	The first letters of the words in the mnemonic are the first letters of the colours in the spectrum *Own answers*	**2(a)** **(b)** **(c)** **(d)**	*Own answers* A suitable diagram showing white light entering the prism to produce coloured lights. A suitable diagram showing coloured lights entering the prism to produce white light. Previously people thought the prism was adding colours to the light; Newton showed that the colours were already in white light, and that you can regain white light by joining them again.
20 What do your eyes need to see things?	**1(a)** **(b)** **(c)** **(d)**	Light coming in through the flap. Nothing. The objects in the box. Light from the source hits the toys, bounces off (is reflected) and goes into their eyes.	**2(a)** **(b)**	Suitable diagrams showing small pupils outside, medium pupils inside and large pupils all the way in. Small pupils protect eyes from being damaged if there is too much light; dilated (large) pupils let more light in so we can still see if there is not much light.

Unit		On track		Aiming higher
21 How does light travel?	**1(a)**	The light could pass through all the holes so you could see it by looking in the hole in card C.	**2(a)** **(b)** **(c)** **3**	300,000 × 10 = 3,000,000 km 300,000 × 60 = 18,000,000 km 300,000 × 60 × 60 = 1,080,000,000 km Mercury = 57,900,000 km Venus = 108,000,000 km Mars = 227,700,000 km Jupiter = 778,500,000 km Saturn = 1,427,700,000 km
	(b)	The holes have to be lined up exactly straight or the light won't pass right through.		
	(c)	You wouldn't be able to see the light through card C		
22 How do light rays move?	**1(a)**	Drawing of ray leaving the lamp and bouncing off the page into the eye.	**2**	C – The light starts in the sun and has to bounce off the tree into the girl's eye. Other pictures take no account of the original source of the light or have the arrows pointing in the wrong direction.
	(b)	Drawing of ray leaving the lamp and bouncing off the boy's teeth into the dentist's eye.	**3(a)**	Drawing of light beam starting at the candle, zig-zagging through the periscope and hitting the boy's eyes
	(c)	Drawing of a ray from candle flame, to flame in mirror and back to girl's eye.	**(b)** **(c)**	Reflection A suitable diagram with arrows showing direction of the light beam.
23 What are reflections and shadows?	**1(a)**	A – The shadow has a lifelike face and it is a different shape to the object from which it is formed. B – The image in the mirror is upside down and it is dark.	**2(a)**	*(see table below)*
	(b) (c)	Suitable drawings, correcting shadows	**(b)**	Shadows are formed when an object blocks light. Reflections appear to be formed on shiny surfaces when light is reflected.
			3	Similar: shape, left/right reversed Different: reflections show lifelike details
24 What can make white light change?	**1(a)**	White light is coloured white – false Daylight is colourless – true Swimming pools look deeper than they really are – false You can only see seven colours in a rainbow – false Soap bubbles are multi-coloured – true The sky at sunset changes colour – true Colour filters are used in theatre lights – true A pencil looks bent in water – true Colour filters let through light of more than one colour – false Daylight contains equal amounts of different coloured lights – true	**2(a)** **(b)**	The fish looks higher in the water than it really is. Aim for a point under where the fish appears to be.
	(b)	1 – White light does not really have a colour at all. 2 – Swimming pools look shallower than they really are 3 – There are many more than seven colours visible in a rainbow – just seven main ones. 4 – Colour filters let one colour of light through		

Table for 23 **2(a)**:

Shadows are formed when light is blocked.	True
Shadows form on shiny surfaces.	False
Images in mirrors are lifelike.	True
Images in mirrors are formed when light is reflected.	True
Shadows look lifelike.	False
Images form on opaque surfaces.	False

Unit		On track		Aiming higher
25 What symbols are used in circuits?	1(a)	A – lamp B – switch C – battery D – connecting wire.	2(a) (b) 3	Battery, connecting wires, buzzer, bulb The lamp lights up Suitable circuits with symbols drawn correctly.
	(b)	A – There should be a diagonal cross in the lamp: it should look like a plus sign B – Should not have circles C – There is a horizontal line missing between the short horizontal line and the long vertical D – Should not be circles on wires.		
	(c)	Symbols drawn correctly as per page 54		
26 Why do some circuits not work?	1(a) (b) (c)	Provide power/make electricity A and C A suitable circuit	2(a) (b)	1 – The plastic spoon is not a conductor. 2 – The switch is open. 3 – The cells are not correctly connected. Suitable circuits
27 What happens when you change the components of a circuit?	1(a) (b) (c) (d)	Motor The circuit with two cells (battery) will go faster. The motors would slow down The motors would run faster.	2(a) (b)	A suitable circuit with symbols drawn correctly. Another cell: The bulb will be brighter A buzzer: The bulb will be dimmer Another bulb: The bulb will be dimmer
28 What happens when cells change in a circuit?	1 2(a)	Suitable circuits with symbols drawn correctly. Number of cells/Speed of the motor <table><tr><td>1 cell</td><td>slow</td></tr><tr><td>2 cells</td><td>fast</td></tr><tr><td>3 cells</td><td>very fast</td></tr></table>	5(a) (b) (c)	D It would be quieter It would be louder
	(b)	The more cells, the faster the motor spins.		
	3	<table><tr><td>Cell</td><td>Number of cells</td><td>Number of motors</td><td>Motor</td></tr><tr><td>1.5 V</td><td>1</td><td>1</td><td>Span round</td></tr><tr><td>3.0 V</td><td>1</td><td>1</td><td>Span faster</td></tr><tr><td>0.5 V</td><td>1</td><td>2</td><td>Did not spin</td></tr></table> A higher voltage makes the motor spin faster, and it is possible to have so little voltage that the motor will not spin at all.		
	4	Adding more cells to a circuit **increases** the brightness of a bulb. Adding more cells to a circuit **increases** the speed of a motor. Using a cell with a higher voltage will **increase** a buzzer's volume.		
29 What happens when you change the wires in a circuit?	1 2	A suitable circuit with a simple cell, connector, a bulb and with a gap to insert different length pieces of wire. A – the question they were testing B – their prediction C – what they measured D – the variables they kept the same E – the variable they changed	3(a) (b)	A suitable description explaining how to carry out the investigation. The thinner the wire, the dimmer the bulb.

On track

1   A boy held one hand up and one hand down. He counted to ten and then put both hands down. He quickly looked at the back of his hands.

The blood vessels looked much fatter on the hand that had been down. You could hardly see them in the other one.

Why do the blood vessels show up much better in the 'down' hand?

- The 'down' hand was hotter.

- The blood had run downwards away from the 'up' hand and into the 'down' hand.

- The 'up' hand was more tired.

Aiming higher

2   Put the sentences in the right order in this chart.

- Our intestines dissolve the food.

- We can move around.

- Blood collects dissolved food from the intestines.

- The muscles use the dissolved food to work.

- Blood carries dissolved food to the muscles.

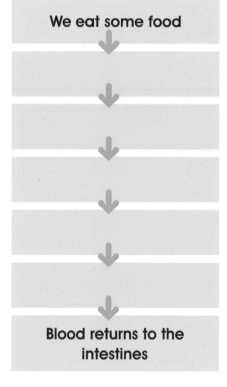

How well am I doing?

On track

I can describe how tubes called blood vessels carry blood.

Aiming higher

I can explain how the circulatory system connects all parts of the body.

15 What does your heart do?

- The heart pumps the blood around your body in the blood vessels.
- **Regular exercise will make your heart grow bigger and stronger.**

Inside your chest, protected by your ribs, is your heart. It pumps blood to every part of your body by beating, which pushes the blood through the blood vessels. It keeps the blood moving round and round the circulatory system. Your heart beats 31 to 42 million times a year.

What does the heart do?

- The heart is made of muscle and it is hollow inside.
- It fills up with blood and then gives a hard squeeze. That pushes the blood out of the heart, making it flow round the body in the blood vessels.
- Each time the heart pumps you can feel it beat in your chest.
- Your pulse is where you can feel the blood rushing along a blood vessel near the surface.
- The heart is a double pump. One pump pushes blood full of oxygen round the body. The other pump pushes blood with less oxygen, because it has been round the body, back to the lungs.

How can I keep my heart fit?

The heart is made of **muscle**, so it will grow bigger and stronger if you make it work hard. Exercise is the best way.

All sorts of exercise and sport are good for you. Even walking for half an hour every day is good for your heart. A good diet is also important for a healthy heart.

You can tell if your heart is fit by taking your pulse.

A strong healthy heart does not need to beat so fast. The pulse rate does not go so high during exercise, and it goes back to normal sooner afterwards. People who smoke can damage their hearts and their pulse rate takes a long time to go back to normal. They are more likely to have a heart attack.

Muscle	Heart rate / Pulse rate
A body tissue that can pull or squeeze.	How many times your heart beats in one minute.

On track

1   The picture shows a human heart.

   (a) What is a human heart made of? Pick one from this list.

muscle	hair	blood	bone

   (b) What does the heart do to the blood?

   (c) What word below means that the blood goes round and round your body?

flows	circulates	runs	beats

   (d) What can you do to keep your heart healthy?

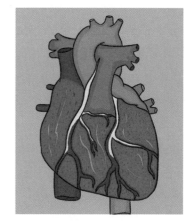

Aiming higher

Jamal and Will both did the same exercise. They were jogging on the spot.

They were wearing heart rate monitors. They go on your wrist like a watch and show your heart rate.

The graph shows their heart rate for each minute.

2   (a) At what time did they start jogging?

   (b) At what time did they stop jogging?

   (c) Whose heart was slower to start with?

   (d) Whose heart rate increased the most?

   (e) Whose heart returned to normal faster?

   (f) Which boy was the fittest?

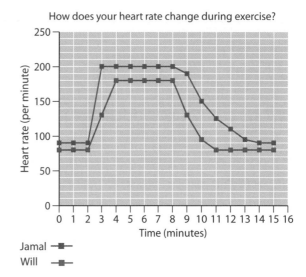

How does your heart rate change during exercise?

Heart rate (per minute)

Time (minutes)

Jamal ■
Will ■

How well am I doing?

On track

I can describe what the heart does.

Aiming higher

I can explain why regular exercise makes the heart grow bigger and stronger.

16 Who discovered blood circulation?

- Early ideas about blood circulation were from Galen about 1800 years ago.
- William Harvey finally understood blood circulation in 1628.

Scientific knowledge can take many years to develop. Scientists living long ago had the first ideas, then others added to these ideas later as they found out more information. People in ancient times had no idea what the heart did. They thought it had to do with feelings such as love.

What did Galen discover?

Galen was a Roman citizen living in the country that we now call Turkey. He lived from 129 AD to 200 AD.

He studied the bodies of dead animals such as monkeys. He cut them open very carefully to look inside. This is called **dissection**.

In Galen's day there were no photographs – but they could make good statues.

Galen found blood vessels and knew they were tubes with blood in them. He did not realise the heart was pumping it round in a circulation. He thought the heart was a 'producer of heat'.

His ideas lasted until William Harvey discovered that blood does circulate.

What did William Harvey discover?

Harvey was an English doctor who lived from 1578 to 1657. He realised the blood circulated in blood vessels, pumped by the heart. He did a famous **experiment**.

He squeezed the blood vessel flat. If he took finger L off first, the blood ran along and filled it up. If he took finger M off first, it did not. In that vessel the blood was always going up the arm away from the hand.

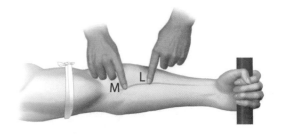

Experiment	Dissection
A way of testing whether a scientific idea is true.	Carefully cutting up a plant or animal to see how it works.

On track

1   Galen lived such a long time ago that the world was very different.
Here are some facts about events in Roman history. They are not in order.

Year 1   Jesus was born.

410   The Romans decided to leave Britain.

64   Rome burned down while Nero was emperor.

129   Galen was born.

61   Queen Boudicca (sometimes called Boadicea) attacked and burned down Roman London.

Draw out the timeline shown on the right and put these events on to it.

400
350
300
250
200
150
100
50
0

Aiming higher

2   Here are some other science discoveries from around the time of William Harvey – and a few other facts, including another fire in London!

1666   Most of London destroyed in the Great Fire.

1687   Isaac Newton formed his theory of gravity.

1615   Galileo proved that the Earth orbits the Sun.

1665   The Great Plague hit London.

(a)   Draw out the timeline shown on the right and use it to put these events in the right order.

(b)   What did Harvey do to show that Galen wasn't correct in his thinking?

1680
1670
1660
1650
1640
1630
1620
1610
1600

How well am I doing?

On track

I can say what Galen thought about blood vessels before the year 200.

Aiming higher

I can explain how William Harvey discovered the circulation of the blood in 1628.

17 How are exercise and pulse rates linked?

- Pulse rate is a measure of how fast your heart is beating.
- **Your heart beats faster when you take exercise.**

Have you ever noticed your heart beating fast in your chest when you have been running very fast? It is pumping blood more quickly round your body. You can count how your heart beats by feeling the blood as it is pumped through your wrist.

What is the pulse rate?

You are feeling the blood being pushed along a blood vessel. Each tick is caused when your heart beats.

Your **pulse rate** is the number of beats you count in one minute.

If you are sitting quietly you will count about 100 beats in a minute.

You can feel your pulse 'ticking' in your wrist.

What does exercise do to your pulse rate?

- Your heart beats faster when you run.
- You might find your pulse rate goes up to about 130 beats a minute.
- It will soon go back to normal when you take a rest.
- The reason is to send more blood to your muscles.
- This lets them work harder.

Heartbeat
You can feel your heart pumping if you feel your chest.

Pulse rate
The number of pulse beats in one minute.

On track

1   Copy this table and fill in the answers.

Question	Answer
What pushes the blood through your blood vessels?	
Where can you feel your pulse?	
What is a normal pulse rate for somebody sitting quietly?	
What is the blood taking to your muscles?	

Aiming higher

Panther class took their pulses. Different children were doing different activities.

Person	Pulse rate (beats per minute)
Dylan	100
Felix	150
Sally	110
Mina	130

2   (a)   Match up each activity to the right person.

Activity	Which person?
Lying down resting for ten minutes	
Sitting in a chair doing some writing	
Walking along slowly	
Running really fast	

(b)   Ms Rankin said that the class should really have the same person doing each activity. Why would that be a better way of doing the experiment?

How well am I doing?

On track

I can describe how to take my pulse.

Aiming higher

I can explain why my pulse beats faster when I exercise.

18 How can we keep ourselves healthy?

● In our ordinary lives there are many risks to our health.

● **Knowing some science helps us make decisions that will help us stay healthy.**

There is a lot we can do for ourselves to help fight off illness and to stay strong and active. Science can show us some rules for healthy living.

What do we need to watch out for to stay healthy?

A healthy diet

Good food gives us energy and builds up our bodies. It contains minerals and vitamins that help us fight off illness.

Exercise

Exercise makes our hearts and muscles stronger and helps to keep us slim. A person who is fit can work harder and keep going for longer. Just going for a walk each day helps you to be more healthy.

Drugs

Many substances are addictive. Once you start it's hard to stop! Heroin and cocaine are very dangerous and illegal. Alcohol makes driving unsafe and harms your health. Smoking damages your heart and lungs.

Lifestyle

Computer games can be addictive! They use up all your time and stop you enjoying friends and family or doing something more active.

What can we do to stay healthy?

Many people find it useful to give themselves simple **rules** to keep healthy.

Eat 'five a day'. Eating five pieces of fruit and vegetables every day helps to balance your diet.	**Keep on walking.** Half an hour walking every day is a good start to taking enough exercise.
Just say 'no' to drugs. Never try any drugs. Stopping is hard; it's much easier never to start.	**Limit screen time.** Two hours of screen time a day is enough – that includes TV as well as computers!

Addictive

Something that is very hard to give up once you are used to it.

Lifestyle

How you live your life: friends, family, work and play.

Test your learning

On track

1   This chart lets us see whether a person is
    the right weight or not. It has been worked
    out for adults, not school children. Don't
    worry if it seems to tell you that you weigh
    too much or too little. It's not about you!

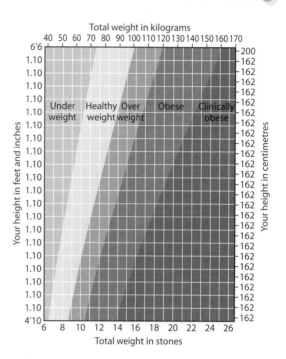

   (a) Ms Rankin told the class that she was
        170 cm tall and that she weighed
        65 kilograms. Is that underweight, a
        healthy weight, or overweight?

   (b) If someone was 180 cm tall and
        weighed 90 kilograms, what word from
        the chart could you use to describe
        their weight?

   (c) What advice would you give to
        someone whose weight came out as
        'obese' on the chart?

Aiming higher

2   You hear someone you know say that they want to try smoking cigarettes to see if
    they like it. They plan to stop later on if it starts to make them ill.

   (a) What would you tell them about smoking to try to stop them? (You could look
        on the Internet for more information to help you answer this one.)

   (b) Why will it be hard for them to stop once they have been smoking for a
        little while?

How well am I doing?

On track

I know some of the everyday things that I
need to think about to stay healthy.

Aiming higher

I know some simple rules I can follow to
stay healthy.

19 What is Newton's spectrum?

- Newton showed that previous ideas of light had been false.
- **There are seven main colours of the spectrum and many colours in between.**

In 1672 Sir Isaac Newton became the first person to show that white light was made up of many different colours. He used glass prisms (triangular pieces of glass) which were very hard to make then. These could separate white light into colours and combine them back into white light again.

What did Newton do?

Newton changed people's ideas about light. In the 17th century people thought that colour was a mixture of light and dark, and that prisms gave colour to light.

Newton disproved this. He set up a **prism** near his window in his rooms at Cambridge University. Light hit the prism and projected a beautiful **spectrum** across the room onto the far wall.

white ray enters

white ray leaves

Newton's prism experiment

To prove that the prism was not colouring the light, he did the experiment in reverse. He projected the different coloured lights onto a second prism. He saw that white light came out of the other end.

What are the seven main colours of the spectrum?

The word spectrum describes the range of colours seen when light emerges from a prism. You can see these in a rainbow.

Newton thought there were seven colours which were:

Red	Orange	Yellow	Green	Blue	Indigo	Violet

In reality there are many more colours that gradually change from one into another. Each letter of ROYGBIV reminds you of one colour.

Alhazen c.1000 AD

First explained that vision is produced by light entering your eye.

Prism

A piece of specially shaped glass used to form a spectrum.

On track

1 Muhammad thought of another mnemonic to help him remember the main colours of the spectrum:

Richard **O**f **Y**ork **G**ave **B**attle **I**n **V**ain

(a) Explain how this mnemonic works.

(b) Think and write down a mnemonic of your own. Add one or two more.

Aiming higher

2 Here are Newton's exact words about his prism experiment. They are written in old-fashioned English.

> 'I procured me a triangular glass prism,... having darkened my chamber and made a small hole in my window shuts, to let in a convenient quantity of the sun's light, I placed my prism at this entrance, that it might be thereby refracted to the opposite wall. It was at first a pleasing divertissement to view the vivid and intense colours produced thereby.'

(a) Rewrite Newton's description in your own words. Add some more facts if it will help your description.

(b) Draw a diagram to show how a prism splits white light into the colours of the rainbow. Use colours in your diagram to help show detail.

(c) Draw a coloured diagram to show how a prism can combine different coloured light into white light.

(d) Explain how this experiment changed people's previous ideas about light.

How well am I doing?

On track

I can describe how prisms split white light into the colours of the spectrum.

Aiming higher

I can tell you the main colours of the spectrum in order.

20 What do your eyes need to see things?

- You see things because light travels from them into your eyes.
- The size of the pupils in the centre of your eyes changes to help you get the right amount of light.

You should already know that the Sun, lights in your house, torches and televisions are all sources of light. You also know you use your eyes to see objects. But how are these two facts related? How exactly do you see things?

What did Panther class see inside their 'peep box'?

Panther class made a peep box. Outside there is a small peephole. A flap lets more or less light into the box.

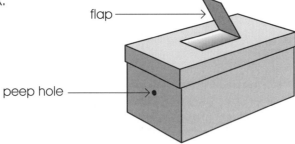

flap

peep hole

When the flap was closed it was dark inside.

When the flap was opened they could see what was inside.

How do your eyes change when more light hits them?

Your pupils get smaller when there is lots of light. Just the right amount of light comes in for you to see well.

Your **pupils** get bigger (dilate) when there is much less light. This enables lots of light to enter your eye so you can see clearly.

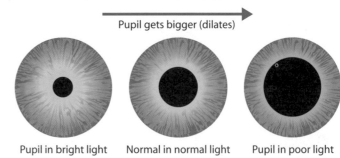

Pupil gets bigger (dilates)

Pupil in bright light   Normal in normal light   Pupil in poor light

Pupil

A black area in the eye where light enters.

Dilate

To become wider.

On track

1   Answer these questions about the peep box that Panther class made.

   (a) What source of light are Panther class counting on?

   (b) What do they see when the flap is closed?

   (c) What do they see when the flap is open?

   (d) Write down which one of these two statements best explains this.

   > Light from the toys comes out the box
   > and goes into their eyes.

   > Light from the light source hits the toys, bounces off
   > (is reflected) and goes into their eyes.

Aiming higher

2   Panther class visited a cave. It was very exciting. They made a story board which showed how their pupils changed as they got further into the cave.

   (a) Draw diagrams of their eyes when they were outside the cave, halfway in and fully in the darkness.

   (b) Explain how the dilation of pupils helps you see clearly and protects your eyes from harm.

How well am I doing?

On track

I can explain how light helps us see things.

Aiming higher

I can describe how the pupils in our eyes adapt to the dark and light.

21 How does light travel?

- Light cannot bend around corners: it travels in a straight line.
- **Light travels at a very fast speed.**

When you switch on a torch you see it light up things immediately. You cannot see the light travelling because it travels so quickly. The first true measurement of the speed of light was made in 1676 by a the Danish astronomer **Olaf Roemer**.

Does light travel in straight lines?

Panther class wanted to test if light travelled in straight lines. Here is how they did it.

The pupils first looked through straight tubes at a lighted candle. They could see the candle clearly.

Next, they looked through bendy tubes. This time they could not see the candle. This is because light passes through the straight tube but is stopped halfway by the bendy tubes.

How fast does light travel?

Scientists now know that light travels at 299,792 kilometres per second. Ms Rankin showed Panther class how to use this to work out the distance between the Sun and the Earth. She used the idea that **distance = speed of light × time**

She knew the speed of light and found out that light takes 500 seconds to travel from the Sun to the Earth. So she used the idea just like this.

Distance = 299,792 × 500 kilometres

That is the same as saying light travels 299,792 kilometres every second for 500 seconds.

The answer is that the Sun is 149,896,000 kilometres away from the Earth.

Speed of light
Light travels at 299,792 kilometres per second. Usually we remember it as 300,000 kilometres per second.

Astronomer
A scientist who studies things in outer space.

On track

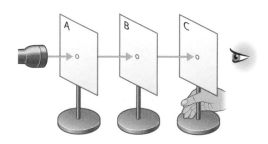

1 Ms Rankin showed Panther class three cards. Each had a hole in the centre. She made sure the holes were all in a straight line.

(a) What would happen when the torch was shone on the card on the left?

(b) Explain how this shows that light travels in straight lines?

(c) What would happen if the middle card was moved so that the holes were not in a straight line?

Aiming higher

2 Calculate how far a light ray will travel in:

(a) 10 seconds

(b) 1 minute

(c) 1 hour

3 Use Ms Rankin's way of calculating to work out the distance of the Earth from the following planets. Copy and complete the table by filling in the third column.

Name of planet	Time it takes light to travel from there to the Earth (s)	Distance away from the Earth (km)
Mercury	193	
Venus	360	
Mars	759	
Jupiter	2595	
Saturn	4759	

How well am I doing?

On track

I can describe a test to show that light travels in straight lines.

Aiming higher

I can calculate how far light travels in a given time.

22 How do light rays move?

- Light rays travel in straight lines.
- **Drawings of light rays help you to explain how you see things.**

Light 'seems to be everywhere'. Light travels so fast that you cannot see it moving. It always travels at the same speed in straight lines. Sometimes the light rays go straight into your eyes. At other times they hit an object, bounce off and then enter your eyes. They can also reflect off shiny surfaces or water before you see them.

How do you draw a light ray correctly in science?

Scientists draw light rays to show light travelling. They only draw one or two rays to make their diagrams clear. Scientists draw **one** arrow in the **centre** of a **straight line** to show the **direction** of travel.

Light travels in a straight line from the candle to the boy's eyes.

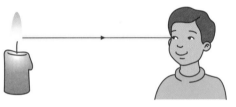

Light from the candle, bounces off the box and travels to the boy's eyes.

How do light beams help you explain what you see?

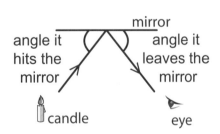

Light rays from the candle are reflected by the mirror before they enter your eyes.

Light from the Sun hits the trees. Some travels straight to your eyes. Some is reflected off the water before you see it.

Light ray

A model of how light travels in a straight line.

Reflect

When light bounces off a surface.

On track

1   Draw light rays to show how:

(a) The girl sees the writing in her book.

(b) The dentist sees the boy's teeth.

(c) The girl sees the candle in the mirror.

Aiming higher

2   Four children in Panther class have drawn pictures to show how the girl sees the tree. Some are wrong! Which one is correct? Explain why the others are wrong.

   A   B   C   D

3   The periscope has two mirrors inside. One at the top and one at the bottom. You can see the candle through it.

   (a) Draw the light ray that goes from the candle to the boy's eyes.

   (b) What name do we give to the bending of light rays by a mirror?

   (c) Draw a diagram to show how mirrors can be used to help you see around corners.

How well am I doing?

On track

I can draw light rays correctly using a straight line and one arrow.

Aiming higher

I can use light rays to explain how we see a number of different things.

23 What are reflections and shadows?

- Reflections and shadows are formed in different ways.
- **Reflections and shadows look completely different.**

Shadows and reflections are very different. **Reflections** are formed when light bounces off a shiny surface. Light rays can be used to show how they are formed. **Shadows** are made when an object blocks some light. An object that does not let light through is called **opaque**. One that lets some light through is **translucent**.

How are reflections and shadows formed?

The girl sees every detail of her face in the mirror. Light rays hit every point of her face and travel to the shiny mirror. They are then reflected back into her eyes.

Some light from the torch lights up the wall. The girl blocks some light, causing the shadow. No light travels back from the shadow and so it looks dark.

How are reflections and shadows similar and different?

Reflections look lifelike.
- You see every detail
- The reflection is coloured
- Its size can change depending on what mirror is used

Shadows do not look lifelike.
- You see no details
- The shadow is dark
- It has the same shape as the object
- Its size can change depending on how it is made

Image
A lifelike likeness of an object produced by a shiny surface.

Shadow
A dark outline of an opaque object formed when light is blocked.

On track

1   Look at these two drawings. Spot what is wrong in each of them.

A    B

(a) Name the two things that are wrong in each diagram.

(b) Draw the shadow in A correctly.

(c) Draw the reflection in B correctly.

Aiming higher

2   Here are some statements about shadows and reflections.

Statement	True or False
Shadows are formed when light is blocked.	
Shadows form on shiny surfaces.	
Images in mirrors are lifelike.	
Images in mirrors are formed when light is reflected.	
Shadows look lifelike.	
Images form on opaque surfaces.	

(a) Decide if each statement is true or false. Copy the table and complete it.

(b) Use ray diagrams to show and explain how shadows and reflections are formed.

3   Make a table showing how shadows and reflections are similar but different.

How well am I doing?

On track

I can explain how reflections and shadows are formed.

Aiming higher

I can describe the differences between reflections and shadows.

24 What can make white light change?

- Light can cause different effects
- **Objects might look bent in water or be multi-coloured**

The ordinary daylight you see is apparently colourless light. It actually contains equal amounts of all the coloured light you can see. Sometimes in nature you can see all the colours again. Water can also appear to make light bend. Photographers use coloured filters to give photographs a special look.

Where can you see coloured light?

Bubbles and water droplets in air cause white light to split into many colours.

Colours form on soap bubbles

Rainbows have many colours, not just seven as some people think.

How did they make sense of their investigation?

The pencil in water looks bent. Coloured filters only let through light of one colour.

The pencil looks closer to the surface than it really is.

Photographs taken with a coloured filter have a coloured tint.

Phenomenon

An occurrence that can be observed.

White light

Ordinary daylight which contains all colours of visible light and is not "white".

On track

1   Ms Rankin gave her class some statements about light phenomena.
Some were true and some were false.

	True	False
White light is coloured white		
Daylight is colourless		
Swimming pools look deeper than they really are		
You can only see seven colours in a rainbow		
Soap bubble are multi-coloured		
The sky at sunset changes colour		
Colour filters are used in theatre lights		
A pencil looks bent in water		
Colour filters let through light of more than one colour		
Daylight contains equal amounts of different coloured light		

(a) Copy the table and put a tick into the correct column to say if they are true
of false.

(b) Select the statements that are false. Write down a sentence which make
them scientifically correct.

Aiming higher

2   This seagull is diving to catch a fish.

(a) When the bird is diving, is the fish
higher or lower in the water than
it looks to be? Explain your
reasoning.

(b) Explain what the bird should do
to make sure it catches the fish.

How well am I doing?

On track

I can describe three things we can see
light doing in real life.

Aiming higher

I can describe what a sea bird needs to do
to successfully catch a fish.

25 What symbols are used in circuits?

- Each electrical component has a special symbol.
- **You can draw electrical circuits more easily using these special symbols.**

Cells, bulbs, wires and other electrical components each have their own special symbols. They have to be drawn correctly. You can use them to quickly draw diagrams of circuits in a very clear way. They can help you to understand circuits and to build your own.

What are the correct symbols for some common components?

These symbols have to be drawn exactly the same every time you use them.

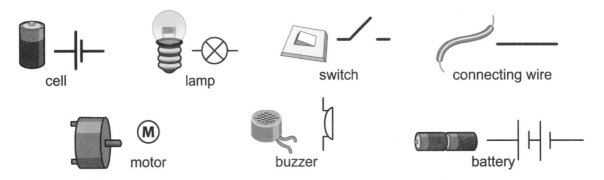

How can symbols be used to draw some simple circuits?

It is important that the wires are shown joined to the components and there are no gaps. Always draw the circuits in a rectangle shape whatever shape the circuit is in real life.

Here are two examples. Both of them have been drawn using the correct symbols.

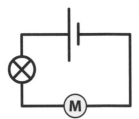

This circuit has one cell, one bulb and a motor. The circuit is complete and both the motor and bulb are working.

This circuit has one cell, one bulb and a switch. When the switch is closed, the circuit is complete and the bulb lights up.

Circuit diagram

A drawing that shows the connected components using symbols.

Electrical symbol

A simple diagram of a component in an electrical circuit.

On track

1 These symbols have all been drawn in the wrong way.

(a) Which component is each one meant to represent?

(b) Explain what is wrong with each component.

(c) Draw and label each one correctly.

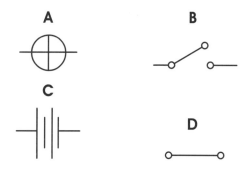

Aiming higher

2 Look at this drawing of a more complicated circuit.

(a) Name the components in this circuit.

(b) When the switch is closed, the buzzer sounds. What else happens?

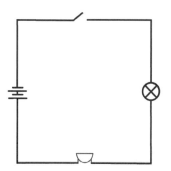

3 Draw the following circuits using the correct symbols.

(a) A battery, two bulbs and connecting wires

(b) A battery, a motor, a switch and connecting wires

(c) A battery, a switch, a bulb, a motor and connecting wires

(d) A cell, a bulb, a switch and connecting wires

How well am I doing?

On track

I can name some of the symbols used in a circuit.

Aiming higher

I can draw a circuit using the correct symbols.

26 Why do some circuits not work?

- Circuits need a sort of electrical 'pump' to make them to work.
- Circuits might not work for a variety of reasons.

Cells or **batteries** are good, safe electrical 'pumps'. Circuits that work all have a power source, materials that conduct electricity, and components like bulbs, motors or buzzers.

How should cells be connected together?

The chemicals in cells make electricity. Cells 'push' electricity round the circuit to make the components work.

Two or more cells, joined together in the correct way, are called a battery.

Circuits do not work if the cells in a battery are connected wrongly.

Always connect the + terminal of one cell to the − terminal of the next cell.

These cells are correctly connected.

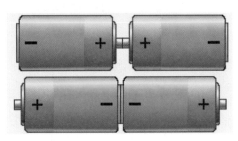

These are not correctly connected.

Why do some circuits not work?

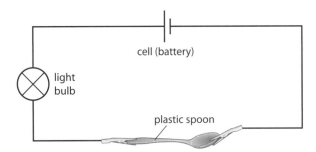

cell (battery)

light bulb

plastic spoon

cell (battery)

light bulb

switch

This does not work because the plastic spoon is an electrical insulator. No electricity can flow through it.

This does not work because the open switch leaves a gap in the circuit. Electricity cannot jump over the gap.

Cell

A device that pumps electricity round a circuit.

Battery

Made by joining two or more electrical cells together.

On track

1 Ms Rankin showed her class a cutaway drawing of a torch. She asked them to look at the components in the circuit and say if there was anything wrong.

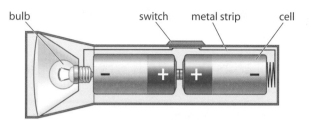

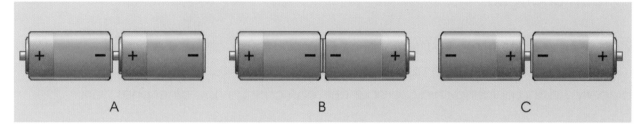

A   B   C

(a) What do the cells (batteries) do in the torch circuit?

(b) Which one of the arrangements of the cells (A, B and C) will work in the torch?

(c) Draw the circuit of the working torch using the correct symbols.

Aiming higher

2 Ms Rankin has made three circuits. Not one of them works!

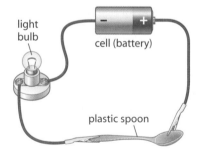

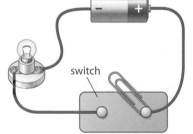

(a) Explain what is stopping the circuit working in each case.

(b) Draw each circuit working and not working using the correct symbols.

(c) Draw two circuits of your own that do **not** work and explain why.

How well am I doing?

On track

I can say what cells and batteries do in a circuit.

Aiming higher

I can give three reasons why some circuits might not work.

27 What happens when you change the components in a circuit?

- Circuits work best when the electric current is big enough for each component to work.
- **The brightness of bulbs, loudness of buzzers or speed of motors can change.**

Cells and batteries come in different sizes. They can 'push' different amounts of electricity round the circuit. Different components need different amounts of electricity to work properly. Adding or taking away components can change how other ones work.

How does changing the number of bulbs affect their brightness?

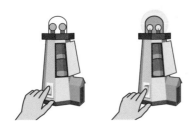 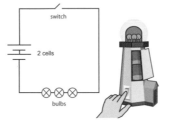 

The two cells push enough electricity through the two bulbs so they light well.

The two cells do not push enough electricity through to make all three bright.

The two cells push enough electricity through to make the single bulb very bright.

Does changing the number of components change the circuit?

Ms Rankin added a motor to her lighthouse to make the lights turn. The first time she tried this it did not work well. So she made some changes.

Adding a motor dims the bulb and the motor runs slower than it should.

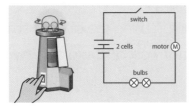

Adding an extra cell makes the bulb and the motor work.

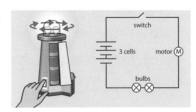

Component

The parts of an electrical circuit such as wires, bulbs and motors.

Circuit

A closed loop that lets electricity flow round. It is pushed round by the cell or battery.

On track

1 Panther class made a model merry-go-round. Inside the model was a simple circuit. They changed the number of cells but kept the motor the same.

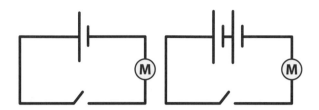

(a) What part of the circuit is connected to the merry-go-round to make it turn?

(b) What will happen to the merry-go-round when the two circuits are switched on?

(c) What would happen to the two motors if you added a bulb to each circuit and switched them on?

(d) What would happen to the two motors if you added an extra cell to each circuit?

Aiming higher

2 Panther class wanted to find out if they could change the brightness of the bulb in this circuit. Each time they add one more component the bulb light ups. They record the brightness of the bulb each time.

(a) Draw the circuit using the correct symbols.

(b) Copy out this table. Tick **ONE** box in each row of the table.

Component used	The bulb will be dimmer	The bulb will not change	The bulb will be brighter
Another cell			
A buzzer			
Another bulb			

How well am I doing?

On track

I can explain how changing the number of cells can affect a circuit.

Aiming higher

I can explain how changing different components can affect a circuit.

28 What happens when cells change in a circuit?

● Changing the number of cells changes how well components work.

● **Changing the voltage of the cells will also change how the components work**

Cells provide the electrical energy in a circuit. Every component needs just the right number of cells to make it work normally. Adding more cells pushes more electricity round the circuit. This means that bulbs will be brighter, buzzers sound louder and motors spin faster. Removing cells has the opposite effect.

Does changing the number of cells change the speed of a motor?

Panther class tested this question.

First, they built a circuit with a 1.5 volt (V) cell, wires and a motor. They observed what happened. The motor spun around.

They did their test again. This time they used two cells and a single motor. The motor spun much faster.

When they added three cells it spun around extremely fast.

Does changing the voltage change the speed of a motor?

They then tested this second question.

They decided to make a simple circuit with one 1.5 V cell and a motor. Again, the motor spun around.

They made a second circuit. This time they used a 3.0 V cell. This had more power. The motor spun much faster.

Then they made a third circuit. This time they used a 0.5 V cell and two motors. The motors did not spin because they did not have enough energy.

Luigi Galvani (1737–1798)

Invented the electrical cell. Special chemical reactions occur inside these and make an electrical pump. High-voltage cells produce more energy every second than low-voltage cells.

On track

1   Draw the three circuits Panther class used when they were testing how changing the number of cells changed the speed of the motor.

2   They made a table for their results of their first test.

Number of cells	1	2	3
Speed of the motor			

   (a) Complete the table for them.

   (b) What does the pattern show?

3   Make a table for the results of their second test. Explain the pattern it shows.

4   Complete these rules. Write them out choosing the correct words.
   Adding more cells to a circuit increases/decreases the brightness of a bulb.
   Adding more cells to a circuit increases/decreases the speed of a motor.
   Using a cell with a higher voltage will increase/decrease a buzzer's volume.

Aiming higher

5   Panther class make a quiz board like the one below. When the wire touches the metal clip, the buzzer will sound.

   (a) Which wire must the metal clip touch for the buzzer to sound?

   (b) What would happen to the buzzer if two cells were used instead of three?

   (c) How would happen to the buzzer if higher voltage cells were used?

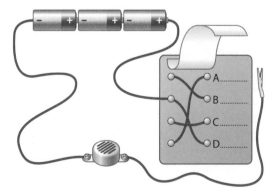

How well am I doing?

On track

I can explain how changing the number of cells can affect a circuit.

Aiming higher

I can explain how changing the voltage of cells can affect a circuit.

29 What happens when you change the wires in a circuit?

● Circuits can show how changing the wires can change a bulb's brightness.

● **Comparisons of a bulb's brightness can help produce a rule.**

Wires in an electrical circuit come in different thicknesses and lengths. They can also be made of different metals. You can alter the brightness of a bulb by changing the wires. However, you must keep your test fair. Your results will help you come up with a rule.

How did Panther class plan their investigation?

Ms Rankin asked the class to investigate the question, 'Does the length of a wire in a circuit alter the brightness of a bulb?'

One group decided that 'We will make our test fair if we compare the brightness of the same bulb in a circuit which has different lengths of same wire.'

What results did they get?

This is what they found out. Can you see a pattern in their results?

Length of wire (m)	2	10	20	30
Brightness of the bulb	very bright	bright	dimmer than normal	very dim
What was the pattern?				

The group decided they could and came up with this rule.

THE LONGER THE WIRE, THE DIMMER THE BULB IS.

Rule

A statement that sums up a pattern.

Wire

A thin length of metal that conducts electricity.

Test your learning

On track

1 Using symbols, draw the circuit that Panther class could use to investigate the effect of wires made out of different metals.

2 Here are some of the ideas that one group came up with when planning their investigation.

A Does the metal the wire is made of affect the brightness of the bulb?

B I think copper wires will make the bulb brighter than nickel or steel wires.

C Let's look at how bright the bulb is when the different wires are used.

D We need to use wires that are the same length and use the same cell and switch in the circuit.

E Let's use wires made of copper, nickel and steel.

What does each statement describe?

- their prediction
- the question they were testing
- what they measured
- the variables they kept the same
- the variable they changed

Aiming higher

3 The class decided to do another investigation. Their new question was, 'How do wires of different thickness affect the brightness of a bulb?'

Here are their results.

Thickness of wire (mm)	5	4	3	2	1
Brightness of bulb	very bright	bright	normal brightness	dimmer than normal	very dim

(a) Describe how you would plan and carry out this investigation.

(b) What rule do their results show?

How well am I doing?

On track

I can set up a circuit to investigate an idea.

Aiming higher

I can use results to come up with a scientific rule.

Index

Adaptation 10, 12
Adaptation 16, 18, 26, 28
Africa 12
Amphibians 8
Animals 6
Arctic 12
Artificial selection 24
Astronomer 46

Bacteria 6
Battery 54, 56
Bipedal 18
Birds 8
Blood 30, 32, 34
Blood vessels 32, 36
Bubbles 52
Buzzer 54

Camouflage 12
Charles Darwin 24, 26
Circuits 54, 56, 58, 62
Circulatory system 32, 36
Classification 6, 8
Colour 42
Colour filters 52

Desert 10
Diet 40
Dinosaur 20
Drugs 40

Electric cell 54, 56, 58, 60
Electrical components 54, 58
Electricity 54
Energy 30
Erasmus Darwin 26
Evolution 24

Exercise 34
Exercise 40
Extinction 20
Eyes 44

Feature 8
Fish 8
Forest 10, 12
Fossils 20, 22
Fungi 6

Galapagos Islands 26
Galen 36

Habitat 10
Health 40
Heart 34, 36
Heart Rate 34
Heartbeat 38
HMS Beagle 26

Ichthyosaur 22
Image 50
Intelligence 28
Intestines 30
Isaac Newton 42

Jurassic 22

Kingdom 6

Lamp 54, 58
Lifestyle 40
Light 46, 46
Light rays 48
Luigi Galvani 60

Mammals 8
Marsupial 8
Mary Anning 22, 26
Mirrors 48, 50

Monotreme 8
Motor 54, 58, 60

Natural selection 24

Olaf Roemer 46
Oxygen 34

Parents 14
Periscope 49
Placental mammals 8
Plants 6
Plasma 32
Prism 42
Protists 6
Pulse rate 34, 36
Pupils 44

Quadripedal 18

Rainbow 52
Red blood cells 32
Reflection 48, 50
Reptiles 8

Sea 12
Shadow 50
Skeleton 28
Smoking 34
Spectrum 42
Speed of light 46
Survival of the fittest 24
Switch 54
Symbols 54

Variation 16, 18, 24
Vertebrates 8

William Harvey 36
Wire 54, 60, 62

X-Ray 30